# INTRODUCTION TO ART SONG

## TENOR

### Songs in English for Classical Voice Students

Compiled by Joan Frey Boytim

ISBN 978-1-4950-6466-1

To access companion recorded piano accompaniments online, visit:
www.halleonard.com/mylibrary

Enter Code
1557-2327-0778-8525

## G. SCHIRMER, Inc.

DISTRIBUTED BY

### HAL•LEONARD®
CORPORATION

7777 W. BLUEMOUND RD. P.O. BOX 13819 MILWAUKEE, WI 53213

www.musicsalesclassical.com
www.halleonard.com

# PREFACE

*Introduction to Art Song* is intended for any beginning classical singer, teenager through adult. In most studios we have students who remain in traditional voice lessons for any number of years. As teachers, this gives us the time to determine the work ethic, the innate talent, and the personality of the student as we explore repertoire. In addition, we often accept beginning students who, for a number of reasons, will only be in our studios for a year or less. It seemed desirable to develop a book of previously successful, well-liked songs in English which are not particularly difficult, yet more mature than the *Easy Songs for Beginning Singers* series for use with these students.

A teacher browsing through the collections will find many familiar songs, but often in alternate keys from what has been previously published. Very often after recitals students will ask to sing a song they heard another singer perform from *The First Book of Solos* series, but it is not published in a suitable key. Some male voice examples: "When I Think Upon the Maidens," "Brother Will, Brother John," "Give a Man a Horse He Can Ride" and "Shenandoah." Female voice examples are "I Love All Graceful Things," "Danny Boy," "The Green Dog," and "Come to the Fair." In my own teaching some of my students will want to have their voice type appropriate volume of *Introduction to Art Song* for access to songs in comfortable keys.

Songs from American and British composers appear which are not included in previous collections. Of special interest are three, short, early songs by Samuel Barber only recently published: "Longing," "Thy Love" and "Music, When Soft Voices Die."

No sacred songs, Christmas songs or spirituals have been included, which makes the collections practical for use in beginning voice classes. The vocal ranges are moderate and the accompaniments are not extremely difficult. Each volume includes 15 to 20 songs.

This final set of four anthologies completes my various compilations of vocal repertoire books for beginning to intermediate singers, which began in 1991 with *The First Book of Solos*.

I want to thank my inspiring editor, Richard Walters, for believing in me, and offering his fine guidance, patience, friendship, and promoting the 60 published compilations, which I hope have made life easier for teachers all over the world. I also wish to thank Hal Leonard Corporation for giving me this amazing opportunity.

*Joan Frey Boytim*
*compiler*

# CONTENTS

Pianists on the recordings: [1]Laura Ward, [2]Brendan Fox

*in memory of my brother, Ralph*

# ACROSS THE WESTERN OCEAN

Irish Sea Chanty
Arranged by Celius Dougherty

say good - bye, Oh, sai - lor, where you __ bound to?

Sis - ters, broth - ers, __ don't you __ cry, O'er the west - ern __

o - cean. Oh, the

times are hard and the wa - ges __ low, Oh, sai - lor, where you

# COLORADO TRAIL

American Folksong
Arranged by Celius Dougherty

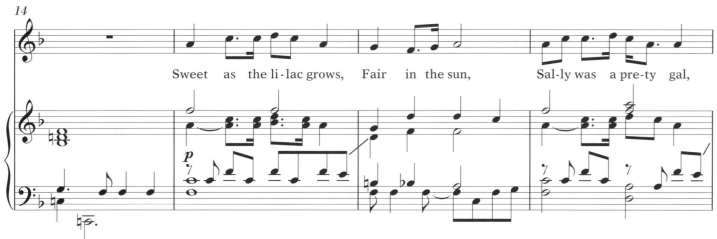

Sweet as the li-lac grows, Fair in the sun, Sal-ly was a pre-ty gal,

God Al-might-y knows. Weep, all ye lit-tle rains, Wail, winds, wail,

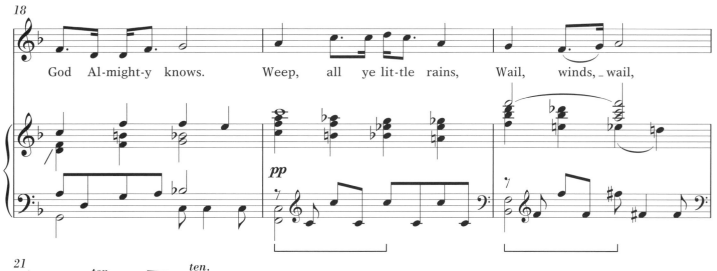

All a-long, a-long, a - long the Col-o-ra-do Trail. A-long the

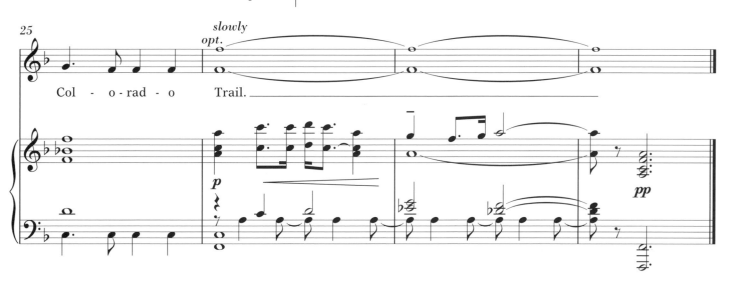

Col - o-rad - o Trail.

# GIVE A MAN A HORSE HE CAN RIDE

James Thomson

Geoffrey O'Hara

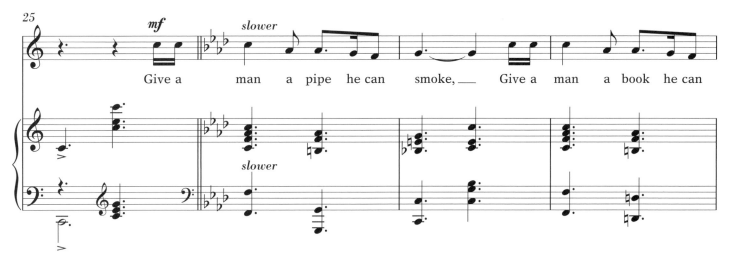

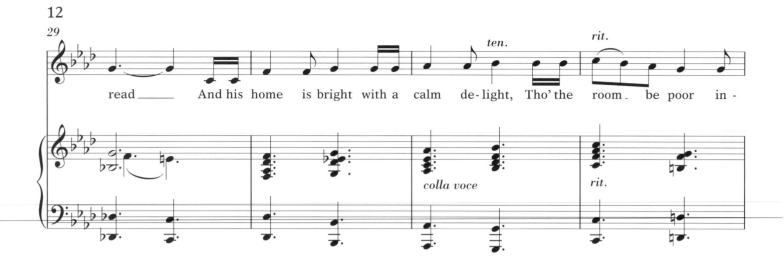

read_____ And his home is bright with a calm de-light, Tho' the room___ be poor in-

deed._____ Give a man a pipe he can smoke,___ Give a man a book he can

read___ And his home is bright with a calm de-light, Tho' the room be poor in-

**Expressivo**

deed. Give a man a girl he can love,_____ As I, oh my love, love

# MOBILE BAY

African-American Chanty
Arranged by Celius Dougherty

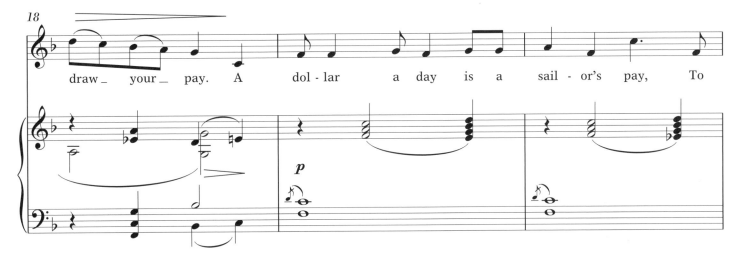

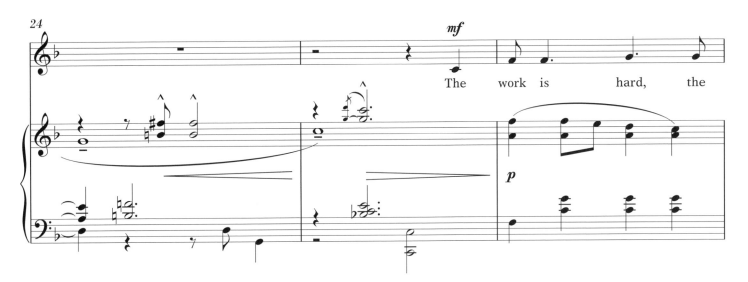

ship is old, John-ny, come tell us and heave a - way, There's

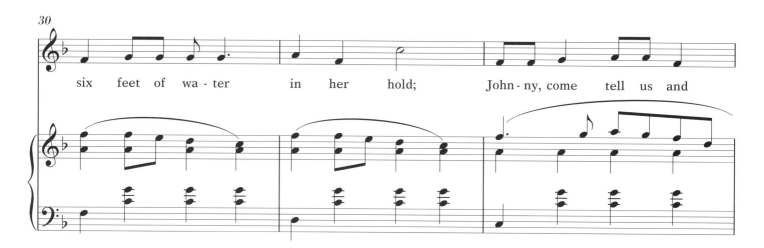

six feet of wa - ter in her hold; John-ny, come tell us and

heave a - way. Aye, aye,___ heave a - way,

Heave a - way, and draw_ your_ pay, The bo-'sun shouts, the

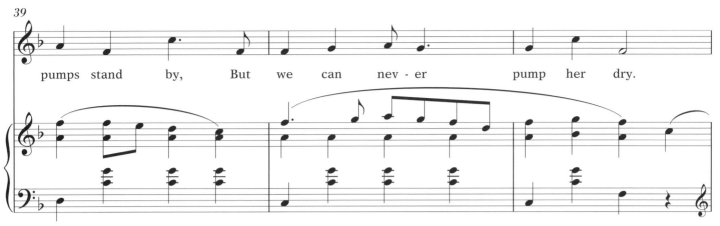

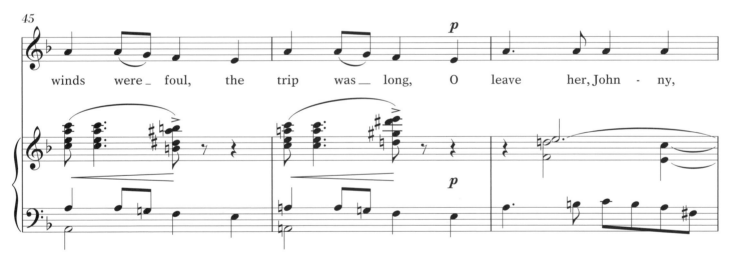

*In this transposed key, the lower F of this chord and its recurrence in measure 58, may be omitted for ease of playing.

time for use to leave her. Aye, aye, ____

heave a - way, Heave a - way and draw your ___ pay, And be -

fore we ___ go we'll sing this ___ song. It's ___ time for us to

leave _____ her.

draw __ your __ pay. The rats have gone, and we, the crew, It's

time, by God, that we went

too! _____

*to my mother*

# BY THE SEA

from *Three Songs of the Sea*

Roger Quilter
Op. 1, No. 3

**Poco allegro con moto** (♩. = 72)

I stood to-day by the shim-m'ring sea;_____ Nev-er was wind_____ so mild__ and free;_____ The light and the love - li-ness daz-zled me,_____

daz - led me. The

waves did fro-lic _____ and curl and roll; _____ They sigh'd and sang _____ to my

list - 'ning soul, And the might _____ of their

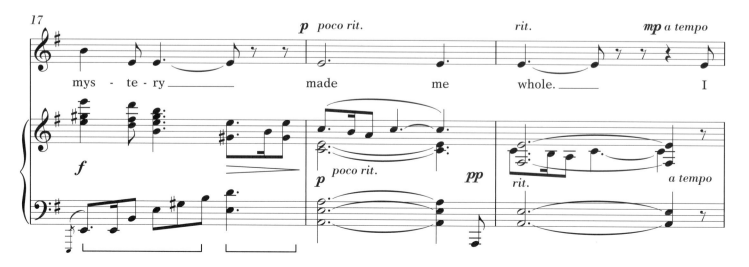

mys - te - ry _____ made me whole. _____ I

stood to-day by the shim - m'ring sea; _____ Nev - er was

wind _____ so mild ___ and free; _____ The

light and the love - li-ness daz - zled me, _____ daz - zled

me.

*to Walter Creighton*

# O MISTRESS MINE

from *Three Shakespeare Songs* (First Set)

William Shakespeare
from *Twelfth Night*

Roger Quilter
Op. 6, No. 2

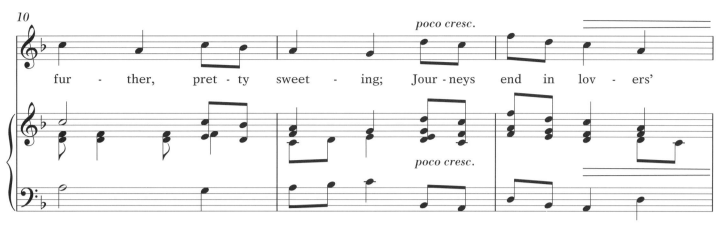

further, pret - ty sweet - ing; Jour - neys end in lov - ers'

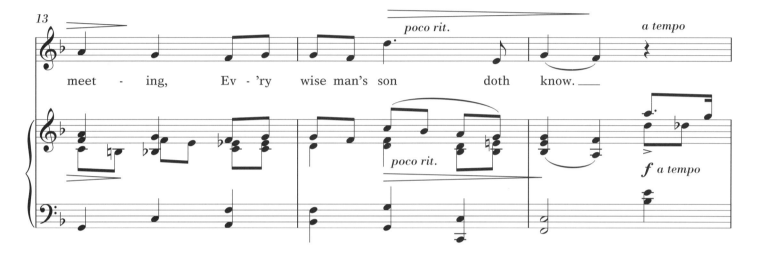

meet - ing, Ev - 'ry wise man's son doth know.

What is

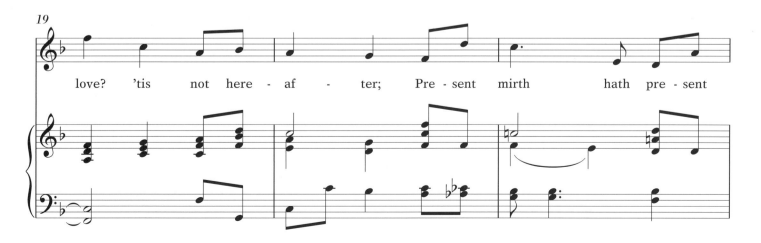

love? 'tis not here - af - ter; Pre - sent mirth hath pre - sent

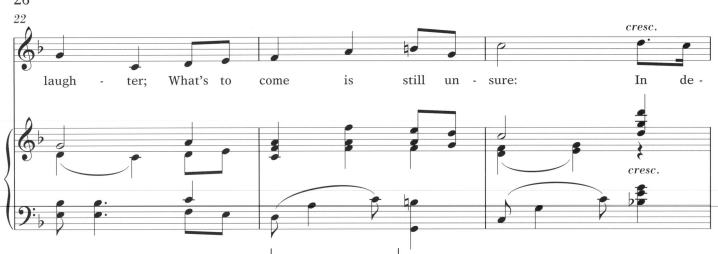

laugh - ter; What's to come is still un - sure: In de -

lay there lies no plen - ty; Then come kiss me, Sweet - and -

twen - ty, Youth's a stuff will not en - dure, not en - dure.

Mis - tress mine, where are you roam - ing?

# THE PRETTY CREATURE

Stephen Storace
Arranged by H. Lane Wilson

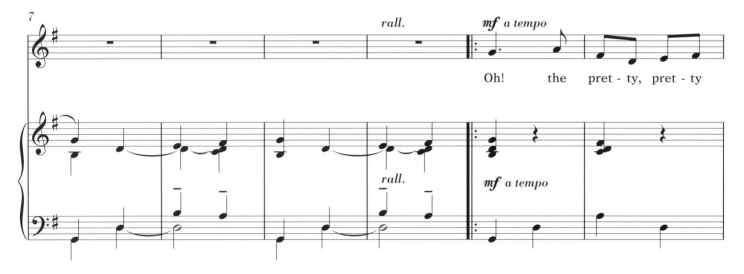

then her wick - ed, charm - ing eyes, When she looks up, show

kind sur - prise; I, like an awk - ward, fool - ish clown,

I, like an awk - ward, fool - ish clown, when she looks up, must

needs look down. _____ Des -

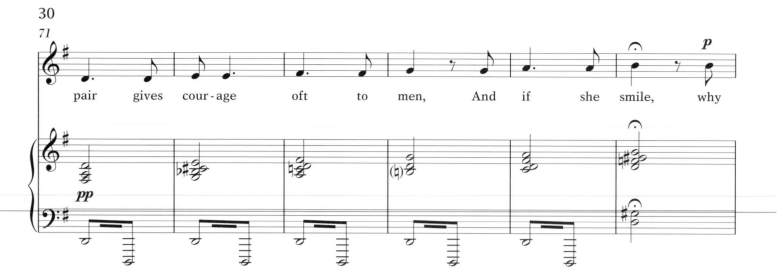

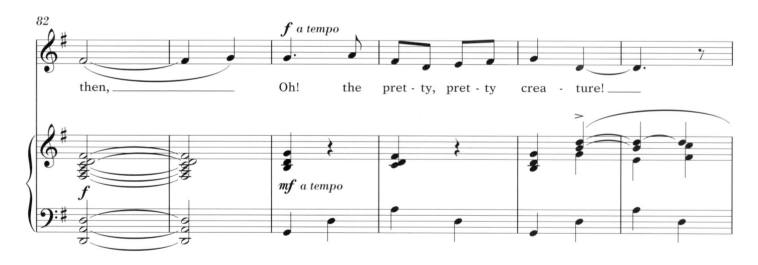

# ROLLING DOWN TO RIO

Rudyard Kipling

Edward German

Yes, week - ly from South-

amp - ton, Great steam - ers white and gold, Go roll - ing down to

Ri - o, (Roll down, roll down to Ri - o!) And I'd like to roll to

Ri - o some - day be-fore I'm old! to roll,

I'd like to roll to Ri-o some-day be-fore I'm old!

I've

nev-er seen a jag-uar nor yet an ar-ma-dill-o

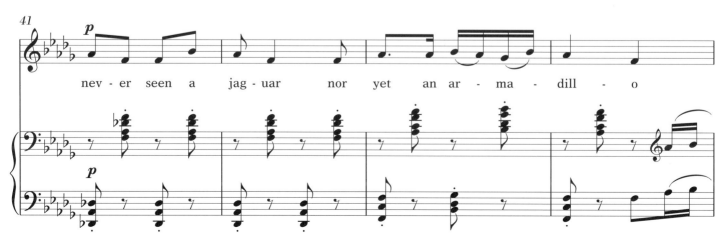

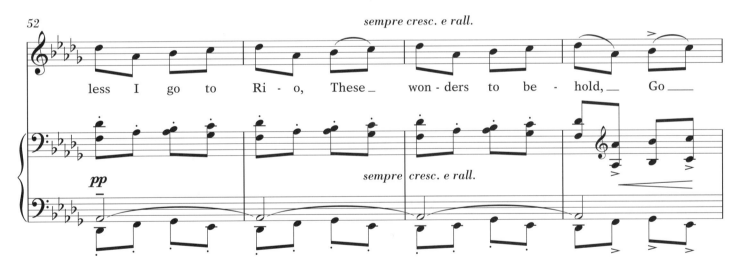

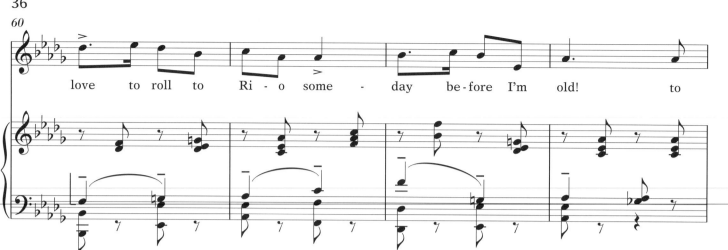

love to roll to Ri - o some - day be - fore I'm old! to

roll, I'd

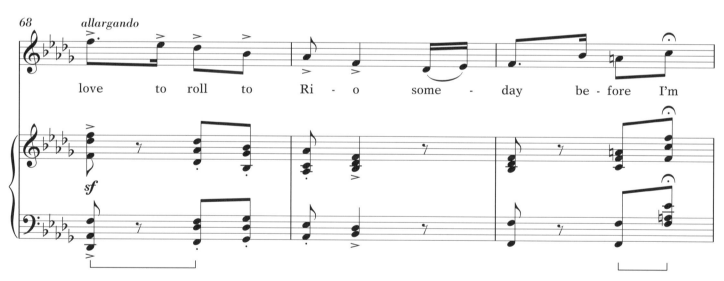

love to roll to Ri - o some - day be - fore I'm

old.

*to my mother*

# THE SEA-BIRD

from *Three Songs of the Sea*

Roger Quilter
Op. 1, No. 1

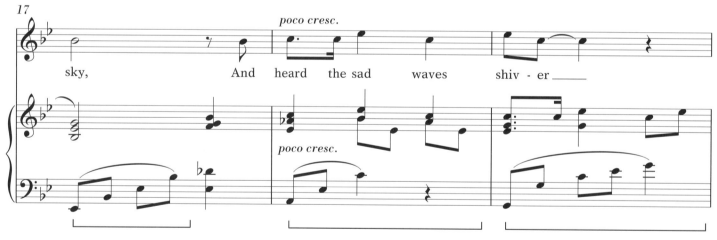

Slow-ly his great wings lift-ing He float-ed a-way a-

lone, Like some tired spi-rit drift-ing In-to the

great Un-known.

# THE ROVIN' GAMBLER

John Jacob Niles

I am a rov-in' gam-bl-er, I've been in man-y a

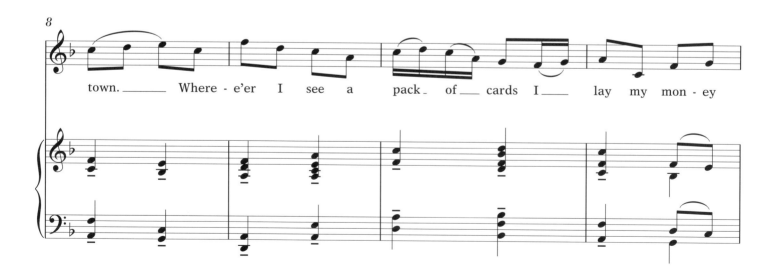

town.___ Where-e'er I see a pack_ of___ cards I___ lay my mon-ey

me. With a click clack oh and a high john-ny ho, And she _ in love _ with

me. We went in the back par - lor, She cooled me with _ her

fan, _____ And she whis-pered soft in her moth - er's _ ear, "I _____ love my gam - blin'

man, _____ I love my gam - blin' man, With a click clack oh and a

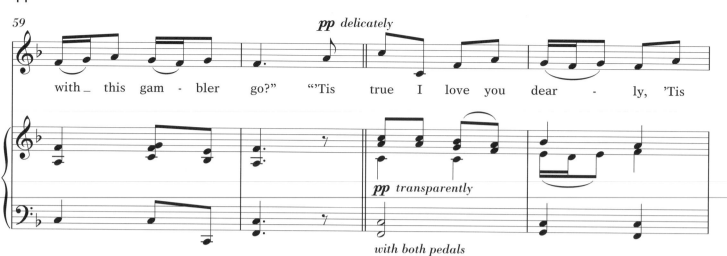

with _ this gam - bler go?" "'Tis true I love you dear - ly, 'Tis

*pp delicately*

*pp transparently*

*with both pedals*

true I love _ you well, _____ But the love I have for the gam - blin' man No _

hu - man tongue can tell, _____ No hu - man tongue can tell. With a

click clack oh and a high _ john - ny ho, No hu - man tongue _ can

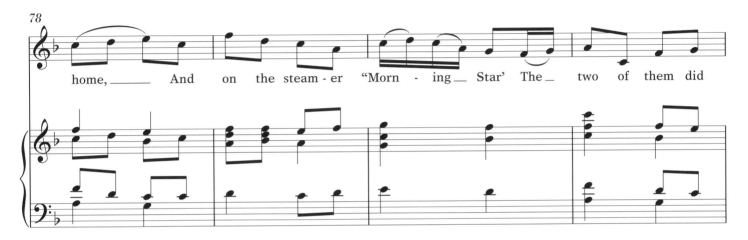

# SHENANDOAH

American Sea Chanty
Arranged by Celius Dougherty

# THE SHIPS OF ARCADY
from *Over the Rim of the Moon*

Francis Ledwidge

Michael Head

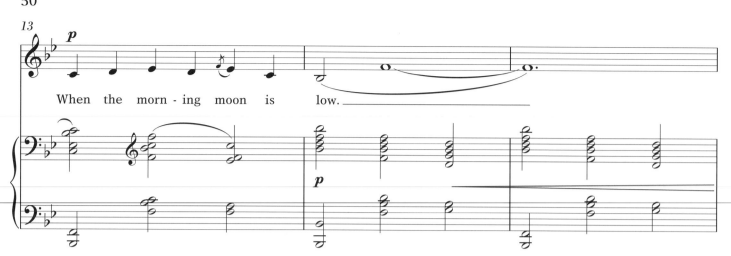

When the morn - ing moon is low. _____

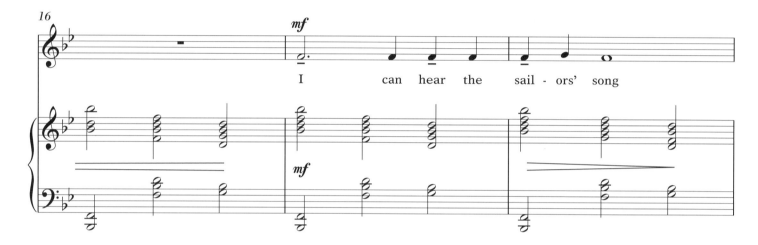

I can hear the sail - ors' song

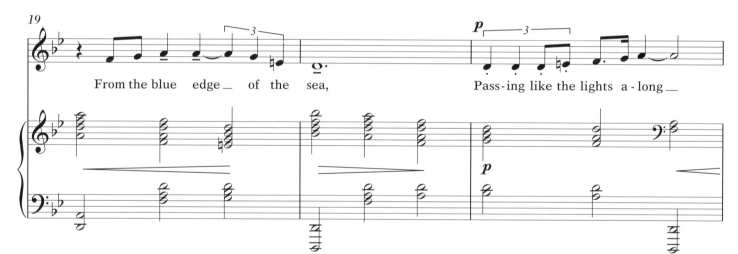

From the blue edge _ of the sea, Pass - ing like the lights a - long _

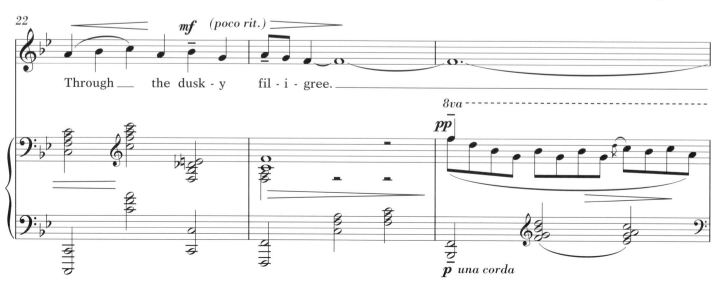

Through _ the dusk - y fil - i - gree. _____

Then where moon and wa - ters meet

Sail ____ by sail they pass a - way, With lit - tle friend - ly

winds re-plete Blow - ing from the break - ing

day. And when the lit - tle

tre corde

ships have flown, Dream - ing still of Ar - ca - dy I

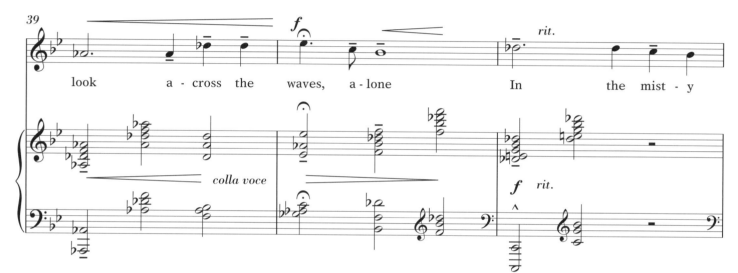

look a - cross the waves, a - lone In the mist - y

fil - i - gree.

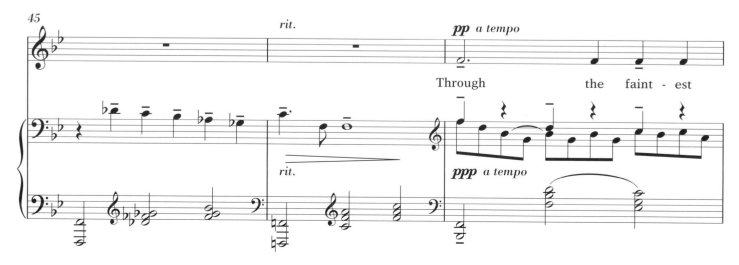

Through the faint - est

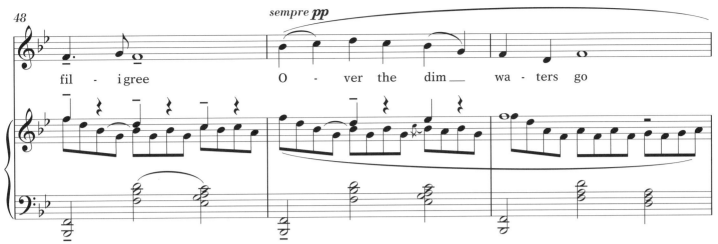

fil - i gree     O - ver the dim___ wa - ters go

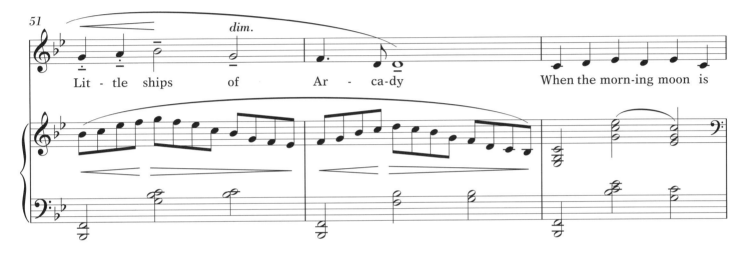

Lit - tle ships     of     Ar - ca-dy     When the morn-ing moon is

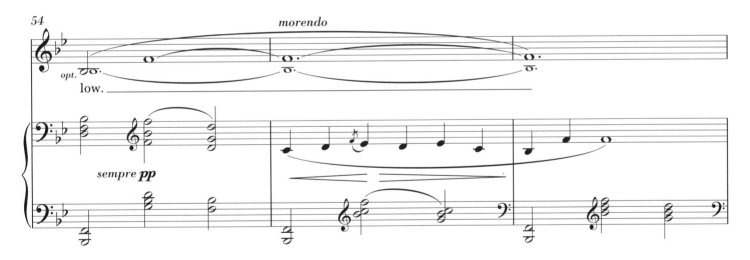

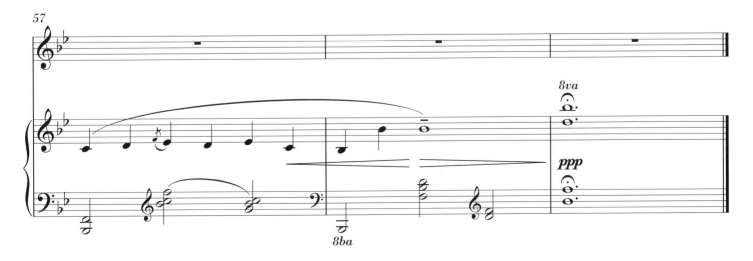

# SIMPLE SIMON

Herbert Hughes

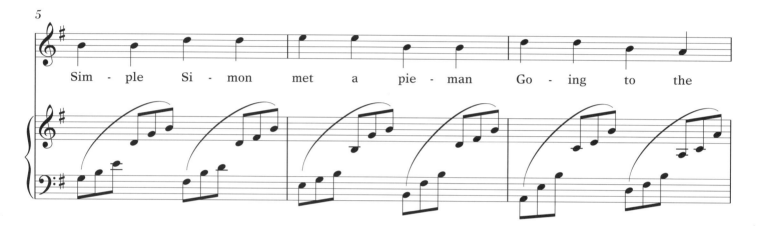

Simple Simon met a pie-man Going to the

fair, Said Simple Simon to the pie-man,

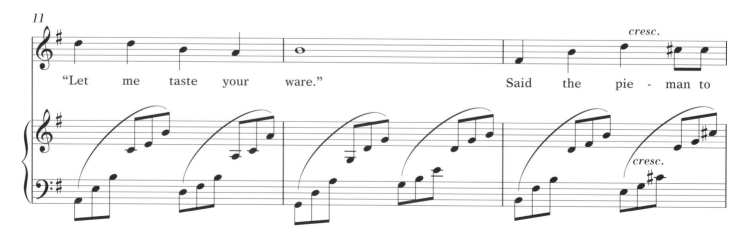

"Let me taste your ware." Said the pie-man to

Sim - ple Si - mon, "Where is now your pen - ny?" _____

___ "A - las!" said Sim - ple Si - mon,

*colla voce*

"I have no pen - ny, ____

No pen - ny." _____

# THINK NO MORE, LAD, LAUGH, BE JOLLY

from *A Shropshire Lad*

A. E. Housman

Arthur Somervell

feath - er pate of fol - ly Bears the _ fall - ing

sky.

Oh, 'tis jest - ing, danc - ing, drink - ing Spins the _ heav - y world a -

round. If young hearts were not so clev - er, Oh they _

would be young _____ for ev - er: Think no more: 'tis on - ly

think - ing Lays ___ lads ___ un - der - ground.

Think no ___ more, lad; laugh, _____

___ be jol - ly; Why should men make haste to die?

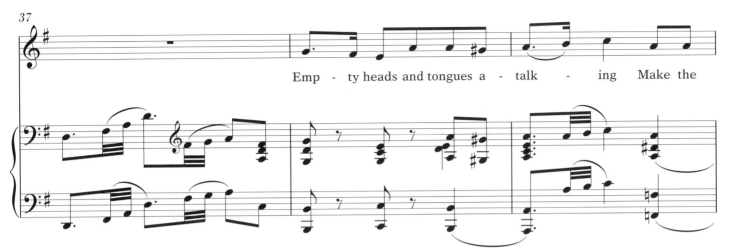

Emp - ty heads and tongues a - talk - ing Make the

rough road eas - y walk - ing, And the feath - er pate of

fol - ly Bears _ the _ fall - ing sky.

# WHEN I HAVE SUNG MY SONGS

Ernest Charles

We've worked so hard to hold our dreams, Just you and

I. I could not share them all a-

gain— I'd rath-er die With just the

thought that I had love so well, so

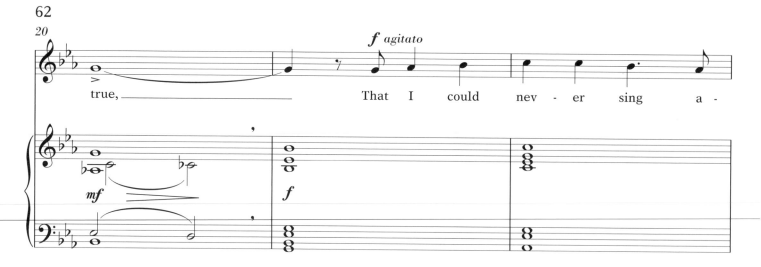

true, _____ That I could nev - er sing a -

gain, That I could nev - er, nev - er sing a -

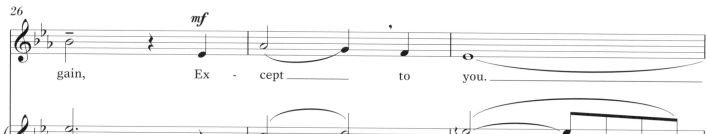

gain, Ex - cept _____ to you. _____